ALBERT EINSTEIN

SCIENTIST OF THE 20th CENTURY

By Catherine Reef

DILLON PRESS, INC.
Minneapolis, Minnesota 55415

Photographic Acknowledgments

The photographs are reproduced by permission of the Albert Einstein Archives, Hebrew University of Jerusalem (The Jewish National and University Library, Jerusalem, call number 40 1576, pages 21, 23, 28, 51, and cover); the American Institute of Physics (courtesy AIP Niels Bohr Library, pages 6, 55, 57); The Hebrew University of Jerusalem (courtesy AIP Niels Bohr Library, pages 9, 11, 14, 18, 35, 38, 44, 46); and Lucien Aigner (page 48). A special thanks to Marjorie Graham, Photo Librarian, Center for History of Physics, American Institute of Physics; Ehud Benamy, American Friends of the Hebrew University; and Ze'ev Rosenkranz, The Jewish National and University Library, Albert Einstein Archives.

Library of Congress Cataloging-in-Publication Data

Reef, Catherine.
    Albert Einstein, scientist of the 20th century / Catherine Reef.
      p. cm. — (Taking part books)
    Includes bibliographical references and index.
    Summary: A biography of physicist Albert Einstein, the man who put forth the general theory of relativity.
    ISBN 0-87518-487-1
    1. Einstein, Albert, 1879-1955—Juvenile literature.
2. Physicists—Biography—Juvenile literature. [1. Einstein, Albert, 1879-1955. 2. Physicists.] I. Title.
QC16.E5R365 1991
530' .092—dc20

[B]   91-7560
                                          CIP
                                          AC

Dillon Press, Inc., 242 Portland Avenue South
Minneapolis, Minnesota 55415

Printed in the United States of America
1 2 3 4 5 6 7 8 9 10 99 98 97 96 95 94 93 92 91

Contents

ALBERT EINSTEIN

Albert Einstein (1879-1955) is the best-known scientist of the twentieth century. His ideas gave people a new understanding of time, space, gravity, and the nature of light. They have aided in the study of molecules and of the movement of planets in space.

Albert Einstein was born in Germany. He lived in several countries during his life, including Italy, Switzerland, and the United States. Einstein was a poor student throughout his school years, but he liked to study science and mathematics on his own. His great interest was physics—the study of matter and energy. Matter is anything that is a solid, liquid, or gas. Energy refers to forces that move or change matter.

In 1905 Einstein proposed his Special Theory of Relativity. According to this theory, people view time and space differently, depending on their positions relative, or in relation, to one another. For example, to a person standing at the exact midpoint between two lamps, those lamps might appear to flash at the same time. But a person passing by very quickly in a train would see one lamp flash before the other. This happens because the light from one lamp would reach that person before the light from the other lamp. Time, then, would be different for the two people.

The Special Theory of Relativity also presented new information about matter and energy. Einstein proved that matter and energy are really different forms of the same thing. Inside the tiniest bit of matter, the atom, was a vast amount of energy.

Einstein's General Theory of Relativity showed that gravity, too, is relative, Gravity is the force that attracts two bodies of matter toward one another. This theory explained that a person gaining speed would feel a force exactly like the pull of gravity. In a spaceship without windows, that person would not be able to tell if the ship had started to move faster, or if it were being pulled by gravity from a planet or star.

Because he was famous, Albert Einstein had many opportunities to speak out about causes in which he believed. One of those causes was Zionism, the movement to create the Jewish nation of Israel. Another was world peace. Many times he urged the nations of the world to get rid of their weapons. Albert Einstein is remembered as a great scientist who worked hard to make the world a better place for all people.

Albert Einstein and his wife, Elsa, traveled to the United States aboard the
Dutch ship Rotterdam in 1921.

•1•

He'll Never Make a Success of Anything

On April 2, 1921, the Dutch ship *Rotterdam* docked in New York City. Thousands of people crowded the pier. They came to catch a glimpse of Albert Einstein, the most famous scientist in the world. Einstein's revolutionary ideas about time, space, and the nature of light had excited people everywhere. They helped to explain the vast universe and the tiny world within atoms.

A welcoming committee of politicians boarded the ship, and a swarm of newspaper reporters followed. The reporters asked the scientist to do the impossible—to explain his complex ideas in just a few sentences. Albert Einstein listened patiently and answered as well as he could. Jokingly, he said, "I hope I have passed my examination."

Soon Einstein came out to greet the crowd. He wore an old, faded overcoat and a black hat. With his pipe in one hand and his violin case in the other, he did not look much like a scientist. Wrote one newspaper reporter, "He looked like an artist—a musician." It was a fitting description, because Albert Einstein did not work in a laboratory, the way many scientists do. Instead, he often worked in his imagination, like an artist or a composer.

Many people believe that Albert Einstein was a genius—that he was far more intelligent than most men and women. Both scientists and members of the public share this opinion. Yet as a boy, the man who would change the course of scientific thinking was a poor student. He did not even begin to speak until the age of three.

Albert Einstein was born in Ulm, a city of twisting, narrow streets in southwest Germany, on March 14, 1879. His mother, Pauline, was a quiet,

Albert Einstein's mother and father, Hermann and Pauline Einstein.

thoughtful woman who enjoyed music and books. His father, Hermann, owned a small electrical workshop when Albert was born. Hermann's fun-loving nature was not suited to business. He found it much more pleasant to go on trips with his family into the countryside. To happy-go-lucky Hermann Einstein, working long hours could not compare to sitting beside a mountain lake or enjoying beer and sausages at a friendly tavern.

Unfortunately for the Einsteins, the country outings were not good for business. The electrical workshop soon failed. In search of new opportunities, the family moved to Munich, a larger city. There the ever-hopeful Hermann opened an electrical equipment shop with his brother, Jakob. This business fared well for a few years, and the family lived in a suburban cottage with a large garden.

Soon Albert had a sister, Maria, who was called Maja. "But where are her wheels?" the curious boy asked his parents. Albert was disappointed at first that the baby was not a new toy, but he quickly grew to love his sister. Still, when she and her playmates would run and play, Albert often went off alone to work puzzles or build towers of cards. "Father Bore," a nursemaid called the serious child.

This is the earliest known photograph of Albert Einstein.

The Einsteins were Jewish, but they were not very religious. They did not attend services at the nearby synagogue, and they did not follow the Jewish religion's strict rules about eating. For instance, they ate bacon, ham, and shellfish, foods forbidden by those rules. Young Albert even attended a Catholic school, because it was close to his home.

The other children sometimes teased the only Jewish boy in school, and called him names. Yet when the Catholic children needed help with their religious studies, they often came to young Albert. The boy enjoyed his lessons in the Catholic faith. They dealt with the fascinating idea that unseen forces—God and the Angels—might control the actions of the world.

But on the whole, Albert disliked school and did poorly in his studies. It was the school's strictness that most bothered him. He did not like standing at attention when the teachers spoke to him. It was unfair, he thought, that the pupils could only answer questions, and not ask them. For a while his parents worried that his intelligence was below normal. The school's headmaster (principal) once told Hermann Einstein that it did not matter what career the boy chose, because "he'll never make a success of anything."

Albert's curious mind was stifled in school, but it developed freely at home. His Uncle Jakob taught him algebra, a branch of mathematics in which letters stand for unknown numbers. "It is a merry science," Uncle Jakob explained. "When the animal we are hunting cannot be caught, we call it X temporarily and continue to hunt it until it is bagged."

Violin lessons helped Albert express his feelings through music. He loved the compositions of Wolfgang Amadeus Mozart best, because they reminded him of mathematics. To Albert, the exact arrangement of their musical notes, like the numbers

and letters of a problem in algebra, added to their beauty.

Once when Albert was sick in bed, his father gave him a compass to play with. As the boy turned the compass in his hand, its needle always pointed north. This showed him, he recalled years later, that "something deeply hidden had to be behind things." In this case, the earth's magnetic field was the unseen force that caused the needle to move.

The boy who liked puzzles when he was younger now loved to read. Through a popular series of nature books, Albert learned about animals, plants, stars, earthquakes, and volcanoes. Another favorite book, *Force and Matter*, explained why a ball that is thrown falls to earth and why a stretched spring recoils, or snaps back into its original shape. It helped him understand why a skater spins faster with her arms at her sides than with her arms outstretched.

These books belonged to Max Talmey, a medical

Albert and his sister, Maria (Maja), in 1893.

student who often visited the Einstein home. With Talmey's guidance, Albert taught himself calculus, an advanced form of mathematics. "Soon the flight of his mathematical genius was so high that I could no longer follow," Talmey remembered.

Albert Einstein, who knew more about mathematics than many adults, did not like school any better when he entered the *Gymnasium* (high school). Again, he thought the teachers were much too strict. The school's many rules prevented students from thinking for themselves. Later in his life, Albert remembered his years as a young student. "The teachers in the elementary school appeared to me like sergeants," he said, "and in the Gymnasium the teachers were like lieutenants."

Albert did not graduate from the Gymnasium. When Hermann Einstein's business failed once more, the family moved to Milan, Italy, to start over again in that sunny, friendly city. The 15-year-old boy was supposed to stay behind in a Munich boarding-house and finish his studies. But Albert quickly grew lonely, and his teachers disliked his poor attitude. He could not bear to stay in school and soon joined his family in Milan.

·2·

If They Are Roses, They Will Bloom

For two years, Albert's school was the galleries and churches of Milan. He found beauty in the paintings and sculpture of Italy's masters, and joy in the voices of cathedral choirs. Yet while he looked and listened, his mind focused on the things "deeply hidden." Even as he hiked through the Italian hills, Albert asked himself, "What would happen if people could travel at the speed of light? What does it mean when we say that two things happen at the same time?"

Soon Albert was nearly grown, and it was time to learn some way to make a living. His father sent him to school in nearby Switzerland. Hermann hoped that his son would become an electrical engineer, but that career did not interest Albert. He wanted to study physics, the science of matter and energy. Matter is

Albert Einstein at his desk in the Swiss patent office in Bern, Switzerland, in 1905, about the time he wrote his first important articles about physics.

anything that is a solid, liquid, or gas. Energy is a force, such as gravity or heat, that causes matter to move or change. A job as a physics teacher would support the simple life Albert wanted. He told his sister about his plans. "All I'll want in my dining room is a pine table, a bench, and a few chairs."

Albert made some friends in his Swiss schools. One was Marcel Grossmann, an intelligent young man with a good sense of humor. Albert still was a poor student. The only way he could pass his final exams was to study Marcel's careful notes!

Another new friend was Mileva Maric, a young woman from Hungary. The two loved music and liked to talk about the great physicists—scientists who specialize in physics. Soon they grew very close. Albert wrote to Mileva, "How happy I am to have found in you an equal creature who is equally strong and independent as I am."

After graduating from the Swiss National Poly-

Albert Einstein as a Swiss student.

technic Institute in 1900, Albert entered the working world. A year later he became a Swiss citizen. But no steady job awaited the handsome young man with large, brown eyes and dark, curly hair. To support himself, he gave private lessons and worked as a substitute teacher. He also found time to have some fun.

Albert enjoyed spending time with one of his students, a young man from Romania named Maurice Solovine. Soon another man joined their group. Conrad Habicht had studied with Albert at the Swiss Polytechnic Institute. The three formed a little club called the Olympia Academy. They took long walks in the country and shared simple meals of sausages, cheese, and fruit. But mostly they talked and talked. They tried to answer questions such as, "How do you know something is true?"

During this time Albert continued to look for a full-time job. His friend from school, Marcel Grossmann, came to his aid again. Marcel helped Albert get a job in the Swiss Patent Office. A patent protects a person's right to manufacture or sell something that he or she invents. It prevents someone else from copying the invention. At that time, Swiss citizens seeking patents had to submit models of their inventions to the patent office. Albert's job was to study those models. Often he had to rewrite the inventors' confused patent applications.

To Albert, his years in the patent office were time well spent. Working on other people's patent applications taught him to express his ideas clearly in writing. And, he said, "It gave me the opportunity to think about physics."

Albert also thought about his close friend, Mileva Maric. In 1903, they were married. Their first son, Hans Albert, was born a year later.

This 1906 portrait of the Einstein family shows Albert, his first wif
Mileva, and their first son, Hans Alb

Although family life kept him busy, physics was never far from Albert's thoughts. After working in the patent office all day, he studied at night and on Sundays. Sometimes he read in a corner of the family's small apartment. Often he enjoyed lively scientific discussions with Michelangelo Besso, an Italian engineer. Albert spoke eagerly to Besso about space and time, molecules and light. He had some new ideas, and wanted to know if they were any good. Besso encouraged his friend to be patient. About those ideas, he said, "If they are roses, they will bloom."

Soon it was time to stop talking about his ideas and write them down. In 1905, Einstein wrote three articles for a German magazine for scientists, *Annalen der Physik.* After reading those articles, scientists would never think or work the same way again.

One of the articles was about light. While Albert was growing up, many scientists were experimenting

Sir Isaac Newton.

with light. The great English physicist Sir Isaac Newton had called light a stream of moving particles. Yet later experiments had shown light to be more like vibrations, or waves. This created a problem. Other waves, such as sound waves, could not travel through empty space. How, then, did light from the sun and distant stars travel through space to reach the earth?

Also, two scientists named Michelson and Morley had measured the speed of light traveling in different directions. Whether the light traveled in the direction that the earth moved through space or in a different direction, its speed was always the same—186,282 miles per second. This did not make sense to the scientists. Light traveling with the earth, they thought, should move faster than light traveling in other directions.

Albert Einstein discovered some startling answers. He wrote that light travels in waves, but that it is also made of particles, called photons. As particles, light could travel through space. Einstein said that Michelson and Morley's results were correct, because the speed of light through space will always be the same. Later observations proved this to be true.

Einstein also studied time and space, which Newton had called "absolute." Newton meant that time flowed in a constant stream. Time's passing was the same for everyone, he said, regardless of location. Space did not change, either. Again, Albert Einstein proved Newton wrong. Time and space, he wrote, were relative. They depended on a person's location in relation to objects and events. This idea came to be known as Einstein's Special Theory of Relativity.

Since boyhood, Albert had performed what he called "thought experiments." He could not do experiments in a laboratory to test his ideas about space, time, and light, but he could test them in his imagination. This bothered other scientists, but not Albert Einstein. To him, careful thinking, based on a sound knowledge of science, was as good as any work done in a laboratory.

Einstein's 1905 articles also contained new ideas about mass, the amount of matter in an object. He knew that when an object gave off light, a kind of energy, it lost mass. Einstein believed that matter was changing into energy—that matter and energy were different forms of the same thing. This is the meaning of the famous equation $E=mc^2$ (energy equals mass times the speed of light squared). This formula told scientists that every tiny atom—the smallest unit of an element—contains a great deal of energy. In 1905, Albert had no way of knowing that physicists would one day release that energy with an atomic bomb.

What a Sad Species of Animal

Throughout Europe, physicists talked about Albert Einstein's ideas. Many could not understand them at first. "Absurd," some commented. "Incredible," said others. But after much thinking and talking, people began to understand that Einstein had made some remarkable discoveries.

It was hard for the scientists to believe that these great ideas came from an unknown patent-office worker. They wondered why someone this brilliant did not teach at a famous university. Yet Einstein continued to work at the patent office until 1909. In that year, he took a job teaching physics at the University of Zurich in Switzerland's largest city.

At last, Albert hoped to have more time for his own studies. But after a second son, Edouard, was

Albert Einstein at the German University of Prague, in what is now Czechoslovakia, where he taught physics beginning in 1911.

born, finding spare time became even more difficult. One friend who visited the Einstein home saw the scientist sitting in front of a heap of papers covered with numbers. The friend remembered Albert "writing with his right hand and holding his younger son in his left." At the same time, "he kept replying to questions from his older son."

As their family grew larger, Albert and Mileva grew apart. He expected his wife to free him from household duties, so he would have more time for physics. She wanted her husband to spend more time with her. Also, she wanted to help with his work.

Historians do not know if Mileva helped Albert develop the Special Theory of Relativity. For years, they wrote that Mileva could not understand her husband's ideas. Although she had studied physics, she had not passed her final exams. That was proof of her weak knowledge of science, the historians said. But in 1988, a new book featured some letters from

Albert to Mileva that had never been published before. Those letters revealed that while they were students, the couple had a daughter who was given up for adoption. Mileva did not fail because she was a poor student. Instead, she left school to give birth at home in Hungary. Also, Albert wrote in those letters about "our theory" and "our work." It is possible that Mileva grew angry because she received no credit for her help with the theory.

As Einstein's reputation grew, more universities wanted to employ him. In 1911, he moved to the German University at Prague, in what is now Czechoslovakia. A year later, he went to work at his old school, the Swiss Polytechnic Institute at Zurich.

Fancy job titles did not impress Albert Einstein. He spoke to everyone, from professors to janitors, in the same relaxed, friendly manner. His co-workers enjoyed his good sense of humor and down-to-earth ways. As one friend remembered, Albert could speak of "concepts such as time or space as matter-of-factly as others speak of sandwiches or potatoes."

Einstein was popular with his students, too. His lectures could be lively, and they often contained good-natured jokes. He tried to be different from the "sergeants" and "lieutenants" of his school years. He urged his students to ask questions and think for themselves. Sometimes he treated students like members of the Olympia Academy. He invited them to cafes or to his home to share meals and long talks. As busy as he was, Albert told his students, "If you have a problem, come to me with it. You will never disturb me."

While he taught at the university at Prague, Einstein first learned about Zionism. This was a growing movement to establish a Jewish homeland in Palestine, a Middle Eastern land where Jews lived in ancient times. In 1911, Prague was the capital of Bohemia, a country that no longer exists. Most of its citizens belonged to one of two ethnic groups: the Germans and the Czechs. Some of the Germans had started calling themselves the "master race." They thought they were better than other people. Both Germans and Czechs were unfriendly to the city's Jews.

Albert still was not religious, but he felt most at home in the Jewish community. As he made friends with Jewish writers and thinkers, he found that he shared with other Jews a history and traditions. Albert listened to his friends talk about Zionism, but he did not join the cause. He was not ready to let politics take time away from physics.

In 1913, Einstein was asked to direct the Kaiser Wilhelm Institute for Physics in Berlin, Germany. It was a great opportunity. Berlin was known as a center of learning. Students from all over the world flocked there to study with the city's famous professors. In Berlin, Einstein could discuss his ideas with great physicists, mathematicians, and chemists. He would receive a good salary and have nothing to do but study.

Still, Albert remembered his unhappy school years in Germany. And he knew that in 1913, many Germans disliked Jews more than the Bohemians did. Even more people in Germany talked about the "master race." Einstein took the job, but he remained a Swiss citizen. Proud of his heritage, he insisted on being recognized as a Jew.

The Einstein family moved to Berlin in April 1914, but did not remain together for long. Mileva had liked living in Switzerland and did not like Berlin. Sad and restless, Mileva took young Hans Albert and Edouard to Switzerland on vacation when summer came.

Soon the sounds of battle started in Europe. World War I had begun, and Germany fought with Austria against France and England. Mileva decided

Albert Einstein at his home in Berlin, Germany, during World War I.

to stay in peaceful Switzerland, at least for a while. But her marriage had been unhappy, and she did not return. She and Albert later divorced.

Back in Berlin, the war made Einstein angry and disappointed. War prevented scientists in different countries from learning about each other's work. Also, Albert was a pacifist. He believed strongly that nations should not fight, and people should not kill each other. To him, the desire to fight was the greatest human flaw. "In such times one realizes to what a sad species of animal one belongs," he wrote.

Einstein was shocked to see other scientists fighting as soldiers and creating new weapons. He thought that all scientists should be like himself. They should concentrate on their work and refuse to take part in war.

Many scientists disagreed with Einstein. Ninety-three of them wrote a "Manifesto [statement] to the Civilized World," explaining why Germany should be at war. Albert had always avoided politics. Now, though, he decided to speak out. He and three other scientists courageously wrote their own "Manifesto to Europeans." They explained why war was wrong and how it harmed science. At that time, few people were brave enough to protest against the German government.

Europe was in an uproar, but even war could not stop Einstein from working. During World War I he completed work on the theory that would make him world famous—the General Theory of Relativity.

•4•

The Happiest Thought of My Life

For Albert Einstein, the Special Theory of Relativity in 1905 was just a beginning. That theory applied only to objects moving at a constant, or unchanging, speed. For the next several years, Einstein performed new thought experiments to learn what happens as objects speed up or slow down. Those experiments led to a new understanding of gravity. This invisible force attracts two bodies of matter toward one another. Gravity causes objects to fall to earth and holds planets in their orbits around the sun.

Einstein did much of his thinking with mental images, or pictures. Creating those images in his mind helped him to develop new ideas. He translated his ideas into words only as the last step. As a small boy, Albert used mental images to learn about shapes—

Einstein delivers a lecture about his revolutionary theories of relativity.

how triangles fit into squares, and what happens when a circle is cut into pieces. At sixteen, he imagined what it would be like to travel along with a beam of light.

In one of his new thought experiments, Einstein pictured someone falling off a roof. If that person let go of an object, it would stay close to him or her in the air. Einstein realized that the same thing would happen in a place without gravity, such as space.

This experiment was "the happiest thought of my life," wrote Albert. It showed him that like time, gravity is not absolute, but relative. As observers speed up or slow down, gravity changes. Einstein also discovered that gravity from very large objects, such as stars, could attract light. It could bend light rays that passed nearby.

Einstein called these ideas the General Theory of Relativity. This theory has helped scientists understand how gravity from stars affects the orbits of planets. It has also helped to explain the strange places known as black holes. These are areas far away in space where gravity is so strong that not even light can escape.

Creating a new theory took a great deal of time and work. While he worked on it, Albert neglected his appearance and his health. He often wore the same wrinkled suit day after day. His shaggy, graying hair usually was uncombed. When he became ill, he was nursed by his cousin Elsa, who lived in Berlin.

Like Albert, Elsa had been married before, and she had two daughters. The cousins became close friends during World War I, which ended in 1918. Happy and looking forward to a peaceful future, Albert became a German citizen. Then, after Albert and Mileva were divorced, he and Elsa married. This marriage proved to be a happy one.

At the same time, scientists throughout Europe were talking about Einstein's General Theory of Relativity. Many did not fully understand it. "Absolute nonsense!" one said. Others did not like to depend on thought experiments to prove new ideas. These scientists wanted to see real experiments with results that could be measured.

Einstein told them that the theory could be proven during a solar eclipse. When the moon passed between the earth and the sun, it would block much of the sun's light. Then light from stars could be seen—and photographed—in the daytime sky. According to Albert, two photographs would need to be taken. One would show the stars in the sky during the solar eclipse. The other would show the same stars at night, when the sun was not present. Careful measurements of the stars' positions in the two pictures, he claimed, would show that starlight passing the sun had been pulled very slightly toward it by the sun's gravity.

An English astronomer named Arthur Eddington read about Einstein's new theory. He knew that a solar eclipse would take place on May 29, 1919. Eddington was eager to take the pictures that would prove or disprove the General Theory of Relativity. The best place to view the eclipse would be in the Southern Hemisphere, far away from Europe. Eddington led one group of researchers to Africa. He sent another group to Brazil.

Eddington's photographs proved that Einstein was correct. The scientists who did not trust thought experiments at last had their proof, and they were amazed. The results, though, did not surprise Albert at all. When a student told him how happy she was to hear the news, he replied calmly, "I knew that the theory is correct."

Eddington's experiment made Einstein famous throughout the world. At that time, people everywhere wanted to forget about the long war. They wanted to read about the great scientist and his ideas, even if they did not understand them. Albert and Elsa

Albert and Elsa Einstein (right) at a tea ceremony in Japan in 1922.

Einstein were honored guests in England, France, Japan, and the United States. Albert received many awards, including the Nobel Prize for physics in 1921.

For Einstein, fame brought responsibility. No longer could he work on physics all of the time and ignore other areas of life. People listened to him, and he had a chance to work for causes that were important to him. He began to speak about Zionism. Albert had seen the way many European universities turned away Jewish students. The Zionists wanted to create a Hebrew university in Jerusalem. This new school would enable many young Jews to get a good education. Also, having a nation of their own in Palestine would mean safety and dignity for the world's Jews.

Many Germans did not like the things Einstein did and said. They were upset about losing the war and wanted to blame someone. They blamed the pacifists and Jews. Albert was both, and people remembered that he had criticized Germany during the war.

More trouble came in 1929, when the Great Depression began. Prices on the American stock market suddenly plunged. Banks closed, and many people lost their money, their jobs, and their homes.

Many Germans grew frightened about the future as economic hardship spread throughout the world. Anti-Semitism, or prejudice against Jews, became worse. A man named Paul Weyland claimed that Einstein's ideas were part of a Jewish plot to spoil Germany and the world. Weyland and his followers even paid people to speak and write articles against Einstein.

While on a trip to the United States in 1933, Albert and Elsa learned that Adolph Hitler had come to power in Germany. Hitler's Nazi party wanted to make Germany a nation of "Aryans." This was the name they gave to members of the "master race." The Nazis fired Jews and other "non-Aryans" from German universities. They burned copies of Albert's theories in public bonfires. For the Einsteins, it was time to look for a new home. It would be too dangerous for them to return to Berlin.

In 1932, Albert Einstein visited his son, Hans Albert, and his grandson, Bernhard, in California. Shortly afterward, Albert and Elsa Einstein were forced to look for a new home when Adolf Hitler came to power.

I Know a Little about Nature

The Einsteins never went back to Germany. They traveled to Belgium instead, but they did not feel safe there, either. They heard a rumor that the Nazis would try to kill Albert. Belgium's king and queen provided the Einsteins with bodyguards. Even so, the couple decided to make their home in the United States, across the ocean from the Nazi threat.

Albert Einstein took a job at the Institute for Advanced Studies in Princeton, New Jersey. The institute had ties with the famous Princeton University. Here he could devote as much time as he wished to his studies. He and Elsa moved into a small, white house with dark shutters at 112 Mercer Street. But these weary world travelers did not live there together for long.

After his second wife, Elsa, died, Albert shared his home in Princeton with Helen Dukas, his secretary and housekeeper.

Elsa became ill soon after arriving in the United States and died in 1936. Albert kept his sorrow to himself and tried hard to settle into his new job and new country. In the years that followed, he shared his home with his secretary and housekeeper, Helen Dukas. His stepdaughter, Margot, and his sister, Maja, also stayed with him. He often spent quiet, pleasant time reading with Maja.

Albert's son, Hans Albert, had become a professor of engineering in California. After living apart for so many years, Albert and his sons were not close. Still, the famous scientist and Hans Albert enjoyed several visits in the United States. Edouard Einstein remained in Switzerland. He suffered from mental illness and later died in a Swiss hospital.

The Princeton University students thought of Albert as a local character. They watched him walk between the institute and home. They saw an aging man with long, white hair, baggy clothes, and no

Albert Einstein walks along a street near his house in Princeton. Helen Dukas is in the yard in the background.

socks. To the great physicist, worrying about haircuts and "unnecessary" items such as socks took time away from his important work.

Most mornings, Albert walked to the institute. He always took time from his work to listen to the many young people who turned to him for help. He gave them advice about their studies or a career in science. At home in the afternoons, he often played music and chatted with his many visitors. They included scientists, Zionists, and people who, like Albert, had fled Nazi Germany.

By 1939, the world was heading toward war again. Soon, Americans and their European allies would be fighting Germany and Japan. Albert Einstein had opposed war in the past, but this time he did not. Hitler's army had seized Czechoslovakia and threatened to invade Poland. Einstein decided that the Nazis posed such a dangerous threat to the world that they had to be stopped.

He learned that some German scientists had discovered it was possible to split the nucleus, or core, of a uranium atom. This would release a great deal of energy—enough to create a powerful bomb. Einstein wanted the United States to develop this "atomic bomb" before the Germans did. He wrote a letter to President Franklin Roosevelt urging him to put scientists to work to build one. Einstein warned Roosevelt that "a single bomb of this type, carried by boat or exploded in a port, might very well destroy the whole port together with some of the surrounding territory."

During World War II, the U.S. government did employ physicists to build an atomic bomb. Einstein was not one of them, even though he became an American citizen in 1941. Some of Roosevelt's assistants thought he was too outspoken to be trusted with important military secrets. The government's plan to build an atomic bomb was called the

Manhattan Project. The physicists worked in great secrecy deep in the desert at Los Alamos, New Mexico. Einstein did not learn of the Manhattan Project's success until the end of the war. He heard on the radio that a new kind of bomb had been dropped on Japan on August 6, 1945.

Atomic bombs destroyed large sections of Hiroshima and Nagasaki, two Japanese cities. Nearly 200,000 people were killed or injured. A few days later, the Japanese government surrendered. After learning about the damage that those bombs had caused, Einstein regretted urging their development. He called his letter to Roosevelt "the greatest mistake of my life." From then on, he worked for world peace. He even favored a single world government to prevent greedy nations from attacking their neighbors.

As World War II ended, a shocked world learned of the Nazi concentration camps. Millions of people, including 6 million Jews, had died at those terrible

Albert Einstein makes a point during a news conference. After World War II, Einstein worked hard to promote world peace.

camps. Some had starved to death, others had died of diseases, and many more had suffocated in gas chambers.

More than ever, Albert supported Zionism. He watched with excitement as the nation of Israel was formed in 1948, and Chaim Weizmann became its first president. Weizmann died just a few years later, in 1952. Israel's prime minister, David Ben Gurion, began looking for a new president. He recalled thinking at that time, "Why not have the most illustrious [famous] Jew in the world, and possibly the greatest man alive—Einstein?"

Einstein felt honored by Ben Gurion's invitation. Still, he turned down the offer to be president of Israel. "I know a little about nature," he said, "and hardly anything about men." Albert understood that he belonged in the world of science, and not government.

Einstein kept working as he grew older, but he made no more great discoveries. In the years after the General Theory of Relativity was published, the study of physics had changed. Younger physicists talked about the "quantum world" within the atom. This world was made up of extremely small particles, such as electrons. Here nothing was certain. Physicists

Albert Einstein with David Ben Gurion, an early prime minister of Israel and one of its best-known leaders.

could only predict where a particle probably would be found. Einstein never accepted this idea. To him, a true understanding of matter could not be based on what probably would happen.

Albert Einstein spent the last years of his life trying to develop a "unified field theory." This single, complete theory would explain gravity and all of the other hidden forces. It would also explain the motion of matter in both the tiny world of atoms and the vast regions of space. Einstein was not successful in this final project, but he believed that he was headed in the right direction.

One of the scientists who helped to develop the quantum theory was Niels Bohr. Although they disagreed, Einstein and Bohr admired each other and enjoyed discussing the quantum theory. Albert kept in touch with old friends, too. In 1953, he received a postcard from Maurice Solovine and Conrad Habicht, his friends from the Olympia Academy. Now old men, the two had met in Paris to share their happy memories. "We are keeping a chair ready for you," they fondly wrote.

Albert never rejoined his old friends. Age and ill health made it hard for him to travel. Also, he had a great deal to do and not very much time. He was

Glossary

absolute—an observation that is absolute always will be the same, whatever a person's position

algebra—a branch of mathematics in which letters or symbols stand for unknown numbers. The goal is to discover the value of those unknowns

anti-Semitism—prejudice against people of the Jewish faith. The Nazis' hatred of Jews is the best-known example

atom—the smallest particle of an element (a substance that cannot be broken down into other substances)

black hole—a region of space in which the pull of gravity is so strong that nothing, not even light, can escape. A black hole may form from the collapsed remains of a very heavy star after the outer parts of the star have been blown away in a huge explosion

calculus—an advanced form of mathematics used to determine how changes to one quantity affect other quantities

electron—a tiny particle that orbits the nucleus of an atom

energy—a power that is capable of moving or changing matter

working on the unified field theory the night before he died of a heart ailment in 1955.

Albert Einstein achieved much as a scientist and as a concerned citizen of the world. He proved that time and space could change, and that matter and energy were different forms of the same thing. He also tried to make the world a safer, more peaceful place.

Did it take a person much smarter than other people to do what Einstein did? The great scientist himself did not think so. "The important thing is not to stop questioning," he said.

But simply asking questions did not make Albert Einstein great. He studied and thought about those questions for many years. Through hard work and creative thinking, he found answers that forever changed people's understanding of the world.

force—a push or pull that causes an object to move at a different rate of speed

gravity—a force of attraction between two bodies of matter. Gravity is the force that allows the earth and other large objects to attract smaller objects to their surfaces

light—a type of radiation, or energy, that can be seen by the human eye

mass—the amount of matter contained in an object

matter—a substance that has weight and takes up space. Matter takes three forms: solids, liquids, and gases

molecule—the smallest amount of a substance that can exist; a molecule is made of one or more atoms

nucleus—the core of an atom. The nucleus contains particles called protons and neutrons

pacifist—someone who opposes war. A pacifist favors peaceful means for settling disputes between people and nations

particle—a tiny piece of matter that may be even smaller than an atom *photon*—the smallest unit of light

physicist—a scientist who specializes in physics

physics—the study of matter and energy, and how they interact

quantum theory—the idea that matter gives off or absorbs energy such as light in particles, or units. A single unit of energy is called a quantum

relative—an observation that is relative changes according to a person's relationship to his or her surroundings

space—in physics, space refers to an area with length, width, and depth. The word *space* also is used to mean the vast area containing the planets, stars, and galaxies

theory—an explanation for events that is based on known facts and reasoning

time—the occurrence of events in order, from past to present to future. Time can be measured, and its order cannot be reversed

Zionism—the movement to establish a Jewish homeland in Palestine, now known as the nation of Israel

Index

About the Author

Catherine Reef is a free-lance writer and editor whose work has appeared in a number of publications. She is the author of two previous books for young people, *Washington, D.C.,* and *Baltimore,* in the Dillon Downtown America series. Ms. Reef has served as the editor of *Taking Care,* a monthly health education newsletter, and she has written many articles for adults on health-related topics.

The author received a degree in English from Washington State University. She is a resident of Gaithersburg, Maryland.